Phantom

Phantasia

Poetry for the Phantom of the Opera Phan

E.A. Bucchianeri

Batalha Publishers
Portugal

Hardcover, © 2014
ISBN 978-989-96844-61

Library of Congress Subject Headings:

Bucchianeri, E.A.
Phantom Phantasia: Poetry for the Phantom of the Opera Phan
1. American Poetry. 2. American Poetry—21st Century. 3. Phantom of the Opera (Fictitious character). 4. Phantom of the Opera (Fictitious character)—Fiction. 5. Phantom of the Opera (Fictitious character)—Literary Collections. 6. Phantom of the Opera (Fictitious character)—Poems. 7. Phantom of the Opera (Fictitious character)—Poetry.

British Library Catalogue Subject Headings

Bucchianeri, E.A.
Phantom Phantasia: Poetry for the Phantom of the Opera Phan
1. American Poetry—21st Century. 2. Phantom of the Opera (Fictitious character). 3. Phantom of the Opera (Fictitious character)—Poetry. 4. Poetry. 5. Poetry in English 1945—Texts.

Also by E.A. Bucchianeri:

Fiction:

Brushstrokes of a Gadfly

Nonfiction Titles:

Faust: My Soul be Damned for the World (2 Vols.)

Handel's Path to Covent Garden

A Compendium of Essays:
Purcell, Hogarth and Handel, Beethoven, Liszt, Debussy
and Andrew Lloyd Webber

Translations:

We Are Warned: The Prophecies of Marie-Julie Jahenny

This book is lovingly dedicated to
my Mother:

Many times you have risen
above and beyond the call of duty,
how can I repay you
for all you have done for me?

Nothing can compare
with your Motherly love,
may God shower His blessings
on you from above.

Thank you, Mom, for everything.

Table of Contents

A Concert in the Theatre

(Inspired by a harpsichord recital by
Malcolm Pround.)

I enter the dim-lit theatre
and escape the dank cold of the day
the auditorium is not grand,
it is warm and inviting here.
I choose my seat with care,
place my raincoat aside,
slide the dripping umbrella
well out of sight;
these inclement reminders
of the world outside
have no place here, no share.
As I settle into the cushioned seat,
I sigh and shake my head,
how few have come
for an hour's reprieve.
Would they rather be
somewhere else instead?
Some stay wrapped in their coats.
others come to be seen,
unmoved by beauty and grace,
unenlightened they shall remain.
For the faithful few
will the mystic veil part:
they too are here and cherish
this secret in their hearts.

The maestro bows to loud applause,
silence descends for several moments,
God's precious gift then begins to sound,
silence departs vanquished
by Harmony´s instruments.

The sweet strains of Music
fill the air,
lightens the heart, mind and soul.
Worries and cares fade away,
lost in the rapturous melodies here.

As I listen, I recall,
images of centuries past,
wondrous, fantastic places appear;
gentlemen, ladies in lace, silks and satins,
in fashions of gilded ages,
swirling in sweeping formations,
around the musicians, around the theatre.

Fair visions the melodies weave!
Each note a beautiful thread,
now, the ballroom of a palace,
glowing chandeliers overhead,
the ceiling adorned by a master's skill,
colours depicting heroic tales of old,
encircled by cherubs and roses,
gloriously ornamented in gold.

The walls are white silk panelling
bedecked with ancient tapestries
the floor laid with intricate designs,
a vast mosaic of marbling.

The windows, swathed in blue
beyond lay beautiful gardens,
through the panes there stand
stately trees and arbours.

A silver ribbon flows gently by,
the river glinting under the moon,
above stars twinkle a greeting
their light dispelling the gloom.

A new enchantment the Muses show,
Nature in all her glory,
I walk in a tranquil forest,
the light filtering down
through the dark greens and ivy.
I yield to the beauty
of this idyllic daydream,
the air scented with lindens and roses,
this picture of Elysium
carpeted with fragrant leaves
and soft velvet mosses.
The sighing breeze
whispers through the leaves,
gently the verdant canopy
sways overhead,
merrily a brook wends its way,
and babbles in its bed.
Woodland animals are at play;
furry foxes tumble under the ferns,
the shy deer graze in a nearby glade,
curious, casting glances,
while sprightly sparrows, tiny wrens
flit from woody twigs and branches.
Butterflies dance a whirling ballet,
bumbles hum among the flowers,
downy seeds waft on the breeze,
songbirds warble from the bowers.

This charming vision fades away,
another takes its place.
Sublime wonders lie in store,
I am shown a regal residence;
a mighty kingdom, an empire
with more grandeur than before
with matchless treasures that rival
great castles from tales of yore.
Curved domes glisten high,
they reach for the golden sun,
an edifice to outshine
Xanadu of Kubla Khan.
Inside are countless realms
and secret ancient depths
where grim, sombre Charon
tends the flow of Styx and
the dark shores of Acheron.
Rising from that lonely place
stands a symbol of redemption:
a rotunda of marble leads to
the Twelve Gates of Heaven.
The Delphic sibyl guards the way,
and gives the pilgrim direction.

Further on a Great Stairwell
leads us up on high,
a caduceus of polished stone,
the ether region is nigh.
Past the blazing salamanders,
and Light enshrined in bronze,
at last, we see the Great Hall,
where the monarch, Music,
holds court regally enthroned.
The Great Chamber is hung
with patterned silks in red,
while colossal angels of gold
sound trumpets overhead.
A swirling ring of colour,
crowns Apollo's chandelier,
every heart enraptured,
by the music of the spheres.

Alas, the finale sounds,
slowly, these visions fade away,
the music ends, applause resounds,
dispelling the last moments of reverie.

The performance,
however beautiful,
like all, must come to an end.
We cannot muse forever,
again to the world we must wend.

I put on my coat, retrieve my brolly,
sorry my visit so brief,
I leave the theatre, and stare
at reality, cold, wet and dreary.
Yet, beauty cannot be forgotten,
Eternal wisdom can never die,
though I return to a sunless world,
Music and I stride side by side,
cheerful, forever a comforter,
my friend, my heavenly guide.

Rouen

One hope-filled night a newborn cried,
But other cries were raised,
In fright the midwife fled the scene,
The doctor stood there, dazed.
The mother let out a pitiful scream,
The father retreated in scorn,
Their future hopes and dreams were razed,
As they looked on the face of their son.

Pity that child who was born near Rouen,
His only crime, to arrive deformed.
In truth, an apt place to enter the world,
The town of a martyr forsaken and sōld.
The martyr's ashes, the heart, the last to be found,
When that dreaded stake had flamed and burned.
In Rouen, an Angel was tortured as well,
His skeletal face, a new freak show sell.
'The Living Corpse' that child was renamed,
To keep countless jeering mobs entertained.
Betrayed, rejected, unloved by his own,
Out to the world the young boy was thrown.
All through his life continually spurned,
Under the gaze of mankind was he burned.

He wandered the earth, the years passed away,
The Opéra at last became home.
'Living Corpse' he no longer would be,
The reign of the Phantom had come.
"A heart whose empire
Could encompass the world,
In the end, be content with a cellar."
Pity that child born near Rouen,
Whose parents should have known better.

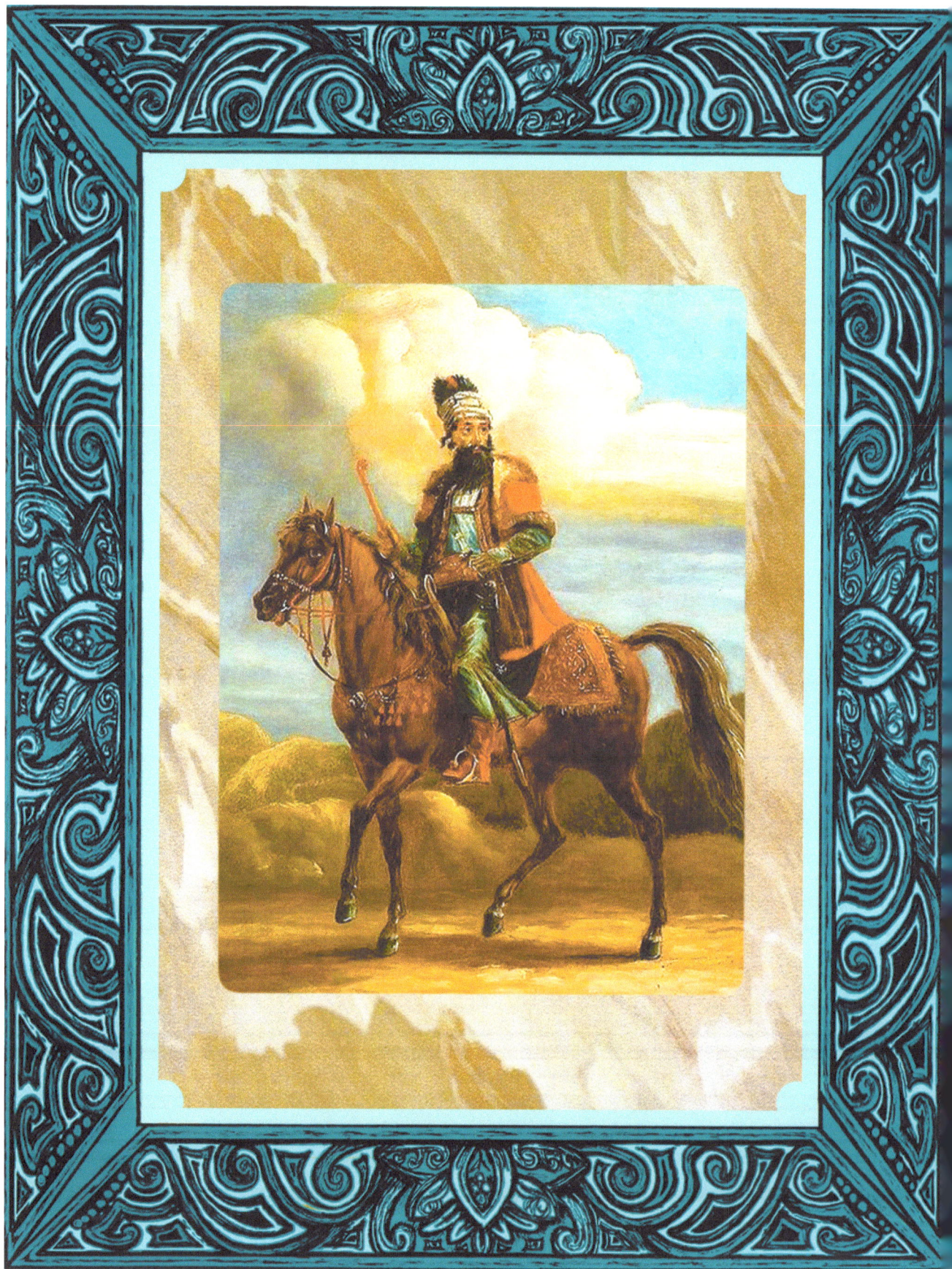

Thanks to the Daroga

You ruthless king,
You horrible thing
To have shown
A tyrannical attitude
Towards Erik who built you
That a wonderful palace,
You should have been filled
With gratitude.

All praise to the Daroga
Who saved Erik's life,
Though his courage and mercy
Caused him much strife.
Thank heaven for Erik's
Faithful friend
Who rescued him
From a torturous end.

The Little Matter of Box Five

"Bonjour, Monsieur,
How may I help you today?

"Bonjour, Madame, I wish to procure
A ticket for the opera tonight,
The critics are singing its praises,
And call it a pure delight,
A splendid production, they say,
Tonight is the last performance,
Whatever you ask, I'm willing to pay."

"One moment please,
Ah, you've come too late,
The house is full for this date,
Just this morning I sold Box Three,
The last place we still had free."

"Oh, is there no space big or small?
No returned tickets for the stalls?
Are you sure there is no box at all?
Why, I'll take a seat in the gods!
May I pay to stand in the hall?"

"I'm sorry, Monsieur, you simply cannot,
It is against the rules, you see.
If only a seat could be bought,
My apologies we have sold Box Three,
Tomorrow night it will be free."

"No, Madame, that will not do,
Tonight's performance I wish to view.
But I know what you can do:
May I be so bold to suggest
Box Five is free and on your list ..."

"Monsieur, you must be mad!
Box Five can never be had
For money, love or the world,
Under strict orders I must keep
Box Five forever on reserve."

"But a friend who attends every night,
Declares to me not a soul is in sight
Within Box Five's silk-lined walls!
Why do you insist on a tale so tall
Box Five is empty, I have no seat at all?"

"Monsieur! You don't understand!
If only you could comprehend
Why Box Five is never sold
And must remain forever on hold
For Whom the eye will never behold ...
You see, Monsieur, l'Opéra is haunted
By a Ghost that watches one and all,
Over the managers he holds power,
No qualms when he wants to flaunt it.
To avoid his curses
They open their purses
And give him a sum, so I'm told.
For every performance,
He demands Box Five,
We don't see the Ghost arrive..."

"Why, this is absurd!
What strange nonsense I've heard!
No time for preposterous fables,
Save odd tales for a dark, cold night
When shadows are cast by the firelight."

"Oh, believe me, Monsieur,
I beg you, please do!
Every word I speak is true,
I can't tell what will ensue
If I sell Box Five to you....
Wait, what is this?
Have they lost their minds?
This time I fear they have crossed the line ...
(Thank you, Giry, that will be all.)
New orders issued, the message is plain,
Yes, the managers have gone insane!"

"Whatever do you mean by this?"
"Tonight's performance you will not miss ..."
"Are you inferring Box Five can be sold?"
"Yes, expect a disaster, if the truth be told..."

"I've grown too old for childish stories
Of curses, genii or witching hosts.
I wish to enjoy the Opéra's delights
To join the other patrons tonight,
Enough, I refuse to believe in ghosts!"

"Box Five is yours, beware Monsieur,
The Ghost will seek revenge.
I beg you, heed my pleading,
I suggest again our upcoming début,
Please come tomorrow evening!"

"No, I cannot! Tonight it must be,
'The patron is always right', you see."
Can you not understand me?"

"Pray tell me your name?"

"Isidore Saack."

"(How strange a name...
He'll be sorry he came,
Will we ever see him
Return again?)"

DIES IRAE

DIES IRAE, DIES ILLA,
SOLVET SAECLUM IN FAVILLA;
TESTE DAVID CUM SIBYLLA.

Lo, the Day of Wrath, that day,
Shall the world in ashes lay;
David thus and Sibyl say.

Oh, how great shall be the fear,
When at last, as Judge severe,
Christ the Lord shall reappear!

When the trumpet's wondrous sound,
Ringing through each burial ground
All shall call the Throne around.

Death and Nature then shall quake
As the Dead from dust awake,
To their Judge reply to make.

Then shall written book be brought,
Showing every deed and thought,
From which judgement will be sought.

Lord, I remind Thee,
Lord, I pray,
I have not forgotten that approaching day.

Alas, I too will know that fear
When the Judge shall draw near.
I wish I was born
With a normal face!
I might not have filled
My past with disgrace.

If only I could devise
A conjuring trick or two
To disappear and escape
This fated rendezvous.

What will I be allowed to say?
Myself, how can I defend?
My crimes cannot be excused away —
I must confess, I did them in the end.

Oh yes, when that book is brought,
My life will appear
As a black ink blot ...

So, before the Judge enthroned,
Shall each hidden sin be owned,
Naught of guilt left unatoned.

How shall them my life appear?
Who the Saint my prayer to hear,
When the just himself shall fear?

Thou, O dread and mighty King,
Mercy's unexhausted Spring,
Now Thy free deliverance bring.

Think, good Jesus, think, I pray,
I it was, that caused Thy way:
Cast me not aside that day!

Faint in search of me hast lain;
On the Cross hast suffered pain:
Shall such labour be in vain?

Oh, how pitiful
Will be that sight
When all I have done
Shall be brought to light!

Will a saint help me
After all I have done?
I would be blessed,
If there were just one.

Yet, in my darkest plight,
Of Mercy's shore
I never lost sight ...

Long before,
My life You could see,
Yet You still consented
To die for me.

I pray this selfless Act
Will not be in vain
For this sinful wretch
Who may fail again.

Who just Judge of vengeance art,
Thy forgiveness now impart,
Ere the accepted day depart.

Guilty, lo, I groan with fear,
Whilst with shame Thy Throne I near:
Thou, O God, my crying hear!

Who didst bend to Mary's grief,
Didst accept the contrite thief,
Wilt not grudge me Thy relief.

I beg Thee to consider
My uncommon circumstances:
Did my life begin
With all the best chances?

Left with an adept and prodigious mind
With a great capacity for good,
The world remained aloof and unkind,
My face was all they understood.

Thus many are my crimes:
Deeds I wish to forget and hide.
I never planned to commit them —
I only wanted to survive.

Yes, I do have a conscience —
Contrary to the judgement of men,
If I were so cold and deliberate
Would I sing my victims´ Requiem?

Though all unworthy is my prayer,
Yet be Thine the gracious care
That Hell's fire be not my share.

Far from that rejected band,
'Mid the sheep O bid me stand,
Safely placed at Thy right hand.

When the cursed at Thy behest,
Go to flames that never rest.
Call me Thou to join the Blessed.

Prostrate now in prayer I bend,
Contrite now my breast I rend,
Help me Thou at my last end.

Sad indeed shall be the day
When the guilty, cast away,
Fall into eternal gloom.
Save us, Lord, from such a doom.

Lord, how can I be saved
After wasting my time
When I should have prayed?

It reads in the *Imitation*
One may avoid all temptation
Refrain from sins that offend,
Keeping death in sight and mind,
Pondering often their last end.

This, O Lord, I have tried to do
That I may grow closer to You,
My method, an eccentricity,
No matter, the prize is all Eternity.

If on thoughts
Of death we are fed,
Thus, a coffin,
Became my bed.

Gaze upon my bedchamber wall:
I have not forgotten the end at all!

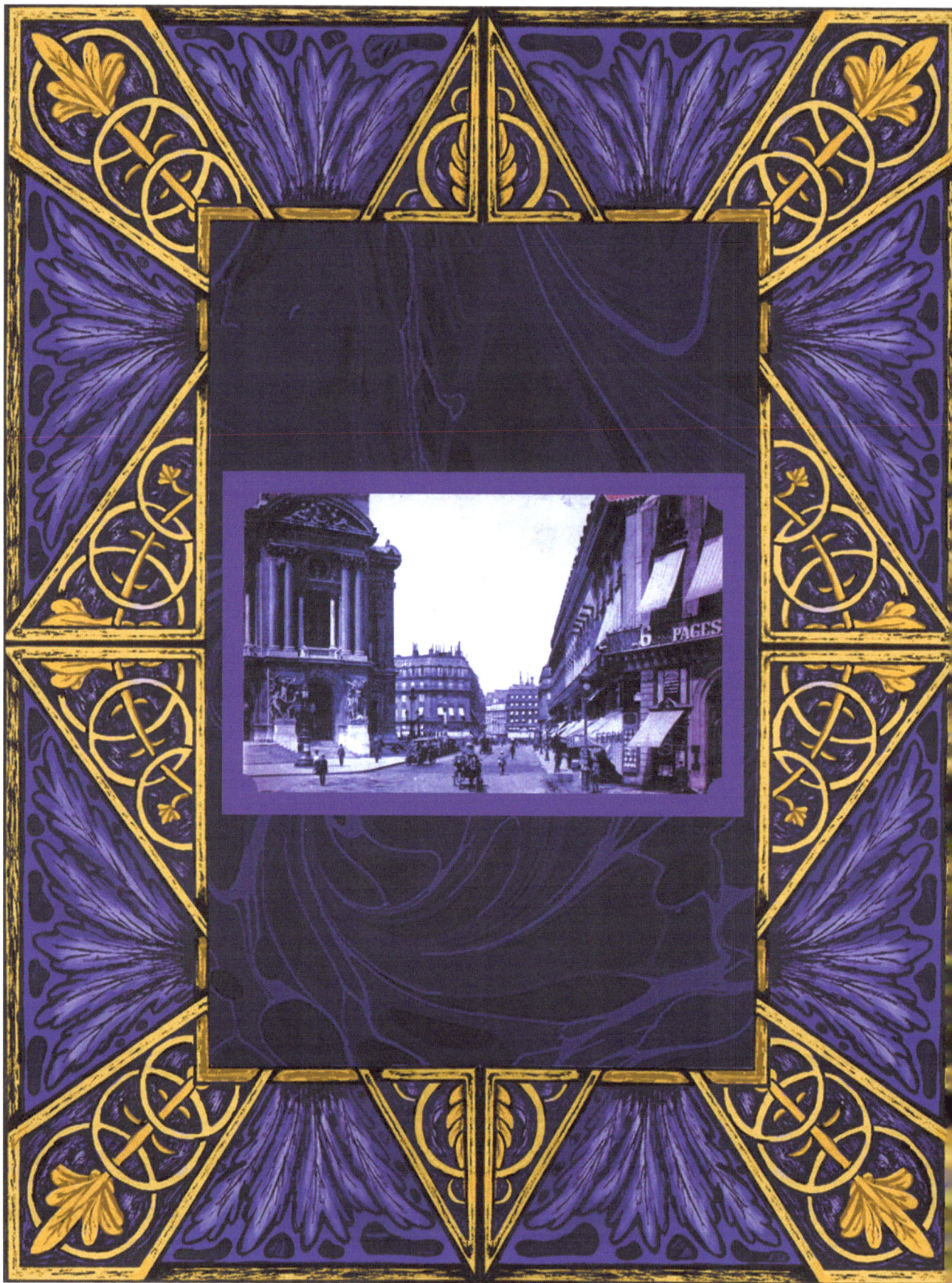

How could I forget my Judgement Day?
I have ever before me the *Dies Irae*.

Thus, shall I quote what Poe once said:

> And ah! Let it never
>   Be foolishly said
> That my room it is gloomy
>   And narrow my bed,
> For a man never slept
>   in a different bed —
> And, to sleep, you must slumber
>   in just such a bed.

PIE JESU, DOMINE,
DONA EIS RÉQUIEM. AMEN.

In Thy mercy, Jesus Blessed,
Grant Thy servants endless rest.   Amen.

One must accept the trials of life
And Judgement shall eventually be,
The Absolute, it is Eternity.

                    So be it.

Music Helps to Forget

Ah, have I reached the end
Of this piece so soon?
I'll play it again,
Music helps to forget
This forsaken tomb
That is my abode
Cellars down
Far below
Under the ground,
A desolate place
Far from above,
Devoid of sunlight
And of love,
The emptiness
Made tolerable
With Music's voice
That helps me forget
The pain here and above,
For the wide world
Gave heartbreak too ...
I'm damned if I don't,
Damned if I do,
A rock or a hard place
Must I choose.
If I live in the world,
I return to derision,
Yet, to remain below,
In Hell I am hidden.

Still, here below
I know I must stay...
It is my grim Fate,
What else can I say?
My life, how vile...
I'll play the organ
Again awhile,
Attempt to forget
These blasted cares,
Embraced by Music,
Melodies and airs.
If only I had
Someone to share
The same love of Music
And its charm
One whom my face
Does not alarm
Their soul
At first sight
Or cause them to flee
Away in fright
They cannot see
The real person, me!
Will I ever know happiness
Here on this earth?
Perhaps through my music,
My last refuge
For peace and mirth.

Fate Links Thee to Me . . .

First Encounter

"What was that?
What did I hear?
Who is speaking to me?
In this room
There is no one I see!"

"Do not fret!
Have no cause for alarm,
I have come to do no harm.
Do you remember
What your father once said,
He would send me to you
When he was dead?"

"No! No! I am dreaming!
This cannot be!
Has father from Heaven
Sent the Angel to me?"

"Yes, Christine! Here I am
To do all in my power
And all that I can
To make you famous
In all the land."

"Oh, it is true,
Dare I believe it?"

"It is true,
My Voice,
Can you hear it?

"Yes, yes I do ...
I am not dreaming.
Am I awake?
There is no mistake ... "

"Yes, my dear child,
From Heaven to you.
Now, listen to all I say,
Your voice shall astonish
All of Paris one day."

My Dear Erik

My dear Erik,
I wish I could be like the few,
A master of all you embraced:
Architecture, music, all the fine arts,
To be graced by the Muses as you.

My dear Erik,
How blessed and gifted in all you did,
When my days seem slow and dim,
These skills do not come easy to me,
My music, elusive and subtly hid.

My dear Erik,
Some days practise ~ hours of drudgery,
Mastering music, an impossible aim?
One step forward ~ two steps behind,
My goals fade, they cruelly forsake me.

But my dear Erik,
You are the Angel, through love, generosity,
Assisted Christine, trapped in despondency,
I beg you, help me, in angelic charity,
Pray my efforts will reflect your mastery!

And then my dear Erik,
With you at my side,
My teacher, friend, protector and guide,
In proficiency may I ever grow strong,
A virtuoso one day with your help to become.

The Carlotta Waltz

(To be sung / recited to the rhythm of The Blue Danube)

Co-ACK, ACK, ACK ACK,
Croak CROAK, croak CROAK!
Co-ack ack ack ACK,
Croak CROAK, croak CROAK,
Co-ack ack ack ACK,
Croak CROAK, croak CROAK!
Cro-ack ack ack ACK,
CO-ACK! CO-ACK!
Cro-ack ack ack ACK,
Ack Ack, Ack Ack!
Cro- ack ack ack ACK,
Ack Ack, Ack Ack!
Cro-ack ack ack ACK,
Ack Ack ACK,
Ack Ack Ack, Ack Ack,
Cro-ACK!

The Dreams of the Phantom Fall

(Inspired by the Kopit / Charles Dance television series.)

How I have waited for this event,
Christine's début, her gala night!
At last my work is done, her voice,
Has reached perfection's lofty height.
No more can this Angel teach her,
Yet, this guiding wing shall not forsake,
My love for her, steadfast, eternal, but wait:
Something is amiss...
What in Heaven's name is wrong?
Her voice? How could that be?
It utters not a sound?
What curse has plagued this house
With malevolence so profound?
The foolish mob!
How dare they jeer and mock?
Beware of the Phantom's wrath!
So be it! A curse fall on them,
These foundations shall I rock!

I slashed at the ropes with hate and despair,
Watched my dreams fall with the chandelier...

FIVE CELLARS DOWN

Are they aware of heartache
Five cellars down?
Have they known scorn like you
Five cellars down?
Have they felt rejection
Five cellars down?
Do they know you exist
Five cellars down?

In crimson robes you vest;
Fifth cellar ····· up!
A cloak of vermilion and gold,
Fourth cellar .... up!
A Death's head for a mask,
Third cellar ... up!
The gleaming scythe is close at hand,
Second cellar .. up!
Resolve and will are set as steel,
First cellar. Up!

Ground floor level ~
Remark the mob's revel,
See how quickly it is stilled!
Like Prince Prospero,
With instant dread was filled!

How could they in their merriment
Forget those who weep and mourn?
Caught up with worldly pleasures
They left you forlorn.

But now you have dared
To come up above;
TOUCH ME NOT!
FOR I AM RED DEATH
STALKING ABROAD!

APOLLO'S LYRE

I have viewed many sights
From the top of the Opéra
At this perilous height,
Paris lies at my feet,
The roof of the Opéra, my throne, my seat.
I watched people come, I have seen them go,
On good days and bad, through sun and snow.

But one mournful night I saw a sight
It froze my bronze heart with dread,
That, if I could, would hang down my head,
For I witnessed all, and heard what she said:
She disclosed *his* secrets and betrayed *his* trust,
She told it all because she thought she must.
How could she know that *he* was there,
Holding onto my lyre high in mid-air?
With a billowing cloak, a great night-bird with wings,
There was he perched, right on the strings.

Alas! What was worse than this terrible thing?
She kissed the other and lost the gold ring!
The pain, the agony! Treachery! Torment!
With his woeful cries, the heavens were rent.
He offered his love … she could not bother,
She gives her love to the other! The other!

True, many tragedies have I seen on this site
Watching from here at this great height,
But nothing compares with that treacherous night.

How Blessed, How Blind

How blessed was she, favoured by the Angel,
She to whom he bestowed the grace
On the secrets of music that very few know,
How I wish it was I in her place.

How blessed was she, his sanctuary revealed,
And trusted with all his secrets,
To be shown the path to the dark, still lake,
To encounter his mysterious existence!

How blessed was she to have heard his voice,
So soft and gentle, a whisper, a sigh,
So melodious when heard, all cares are forgotten,
Music and legends of times gone by.

How blessed, he bestowed to her his love,
More precious than gems or gold,
Hauntingly beautiful, a majestic red rose,
If only that bloom was mine to hold.

How blind was she who could not see
The graces she had been given,
Fear of his face had lost her the grace
And could not partake of these blessings.
Alas, all she saw was human deformity,
Turned her away from hidden treasures within
His opera, his life, would be very different
If in her time and place I had been.
How sad, the rejection, heartache, his pain,
Her love, her feelings so shallow towards him.
True beauty lies not upon gilded veneers,
But found in the soul within.

A Jest with Leroux

Oh, Leroux, you old ghoul
You penned Erik's life a travesty.
Why did you let that fool, Raoul,
Feature too much in the story?

Why did you leave hardly a clue
Of Erik's mysterious life?
Kay had to do it, you went and blew it,
Why go and cause us this strife?

If I were you, my dear Leroux,
I would change the story a tad or two,
Make sure it ended quite differently.
Christine would be faithful and true,
And know what to do:
Erik the one she would marry.

Raoul would meet an end so cruel
It could certainly make one faint:
I think he might die of the pox,
If he survived the 'hot box',
Or what, a bad dose of scurvy?
But Leroux, it was thoughtful of you,
Erik settled the score with Carlotta ~ cro-ack!
She could have turned blue, or died from the flu,
Erik's revenge was poetic, really.

Now Leroux, what think you
Of this twist to the story?
You would not approve, that much is true,
But, I could not change it, honestly.

Ah poor Leroux, I jest with you,
Please understand a number of Phans
Want Raoul to suffer rejection,
Erik deserved to be happy, you see,
Rewrite his life in a bright new direction.

Bad POTO Versions

How I detest a bad POTO version!
Against them I hold a mighty aversion,
When a bad musical or screenplay is made,
We all know what has and will be said:
"They portray Erik not as he was,
They write a villain bent on murder because
With a devil's face he deserved that dark place
In the underground cellars to live ..."
Is that the best these producers can give?
There is more to his story and we are sorry
They don't bother to make it known.
Erik's genius, his passion, his life of pain,
Unimportant to *them*, and rarely shown.

He was not really cruel, but driven by Raoul,
Desperate to win Christine's love,
And perhaps again brave life above,
To escape his haunted, perpetual night,
Out of his darkness and into the light.
For love conquers all as the poets say,
No longer to fear the light of day.
If for years he was forced to kill,
To protect the peace he longed for.
Many an intruder sought that door
To his sanctuary in the cellar,
And if discovered, once more on display
This time, maybe forever,
By those who used him in his youth
Hawking tickets from a booth,
Market his deformity to the crowd,
How could this cruelty be allowed?

And now barbarity plays out again
When they fail to tell his story plain.
Why not adhere to the original book
Refrain from impish temptations to look
For novel absurdities, monstrous grotesqueries,
Developing plots that are just a mockery.
Now we appeal to the world at large,
To writers of books, plays and poetry,
Discover the secret, Erik's heart and soul,
And if you succeed, use that for your goal.

Phans, praise good versions, let those have the glory
Who searched their hearts and found Erik's story.
If Erik existed and lived life in despair,
We wish him to know we are here and we care.

The Daroga's Warning

Remember that line Dante once said?
"Abandon all hope, ye who enter here,"
Of the Opéra's cellars, the same you should dread.
Whatever you do, venture downward with fear.

If you enter there with no invitation,
You risk unleashing the Ghost's vexation,
Stay away from the underground lake I implore,
The Siren will see you are heard of no more.

My advice applies to the third cellar as well,
The wall entrance leads to a very long fall,
That ends in a pit hotter than Hell,
Where no one above can hear you call.

Trusted friends may go where many fear to tread,
If a friend you are not, you'll soon be found dead.

The Eleventh Hour

One says 'Yes',
The other says 'No',
The Scorpion?
The Grasshopper?
Which way will she go?

The Wedding Mass?
The Requiem?
What shall it be?
Nuptials at the Madeleine,
Or flames to eternity?

One says 'Oui',
The other says 'Non,'
Wedding bells?
Funeral knells?
The Opéra blown
To Kingdom Come?

Will she turn the Scorpion,
Or the Sauterelle?
The eleventh hour has come,
Which one of us can tell?

One says 'Yes',
The other says 'No',
The Scorpion,
The Grasshopper?
Which way will she go?

Erik est Mort

(Inspired by the Kopit / Charles Dance television series.)

Many have misunderstood me,
They drown the truth with their fears,
Breathing my last, I lay dying,
My father's arms entwined, Christine's hand in mine,
I feel the warmth of her tears.

Many have misunderstood me,
My love for Christine all consuming,
I killed to protect her, in fear for my life,
My face has always brought strife.

Many have misunderstood me,
My face beckoned the Angel of Death,
Through the heart my father shot me
To which I gave my consent,
To die at the hand of my father,
Is it love, his pity, intent?
Could it be Nemesis, Heaven sent?

The Mask and the Rose

The mask; to hide the ugliness, the pain,
The rose; a token of love,
The mask is no more,
The red rose remains,
You rest with the angels above.

To Impress a Phan Girl
(Erik's Advice)

Your lady love, a 'Phan Girl' you say,
You wish to win her heart?
May I offer sage advice, young man?
A magnanimous head start.
Learn to master the languages,
That's sure to impress her a bit,
Study art and architecture,
That may also prove a hit.
A Grand Tour of the exotic lands
She may not consider too bland.
How is your C.V. these days?
Have you been in the service of kings?
No? Well then, the sooner the better,
They are fascinated by regal things.
Ah yes, a passionate love of music,
Many instruments learn to play:
Violin, harp, piano and organ,
Practise several hours a day.
I don't suppose you have the skill to compose?
Symphonies? Operas? Masses? Quartets?
No matter son, you have some time,
To master those things yet.

And then, do not forget your voice!
Is it sonorous, hypnotic, angelic?
I know with that there is no choice,
Work with Nature's lot for you,
Elocution lessons will have to do.
Not all can sing bel canto.
A mask you ask? Optional I find!
Masks lend appeal of a mysterious kind.
Wait, how careless, I quite forgot,
The most alluring of the lot!
They appreciate a gentleman
Who always dresses for the part,
A finishing touch, an elegant cloak...
Oh, friend, did I hear you choke?
I must agree the list goes on,
But follow to the letter,
You'll win her 'ere long.
To be sure I'm not mad,
There's more I could add...
'Who could pass that test?'
'Too much!' you protest?
Then I bid you good day,
You have it your way.
I revealed what they want.
It's me, don't you see?
A polymath, a Phantom:
Don Juan Triumphant!

Illustrations

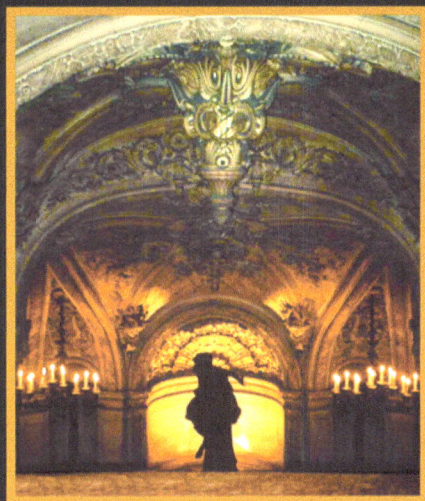

www.ingramcontent.com/pod-product-compliance
Lightning Source LLC
Chambersburg PA
CBHW041954100426
42812CB00018B/2654